SHY GUIDES

QUIET CONFIDENCE

The Shy Guide to Using Your Strengths

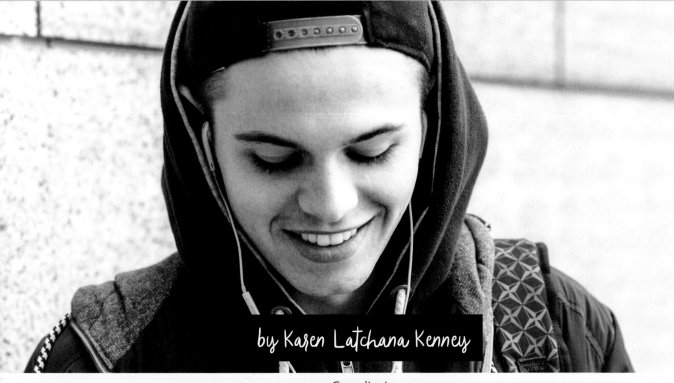

by Karen Latchana Kenney

Consultant:
Christopher A. Flessner, Ph.D.
Associate Professor, Department of Psychological Sciences
Director, Pediatric Anxiety Research Clinic (PARC)
Kent State University
Kent, Ohio

COMPASS POINT BOOKS
a capstone imprint

Compass Point Books are published by Capstone
1710 Roe Crest Drive, North Mankato, Minnesota 56003
www.mycapstone.com

Library of Congress Cataloging-in-Publication Data
Cataloging-in-Publication Data is on file with the Library
of Congress.
ISBN: 978-0-7565-6021-8 (library binding)
ISBN: 978-0-7565-6025-6 (paperback)
ISBN: 978-0-7565-6029-4 (eBook PDF)

Editorial Credits
Abby Colich, editor; Kay Fraser, designer;
Morgan Walters, media researcher; Laura Manthe,
production specialist

Image Credits
Dreamstime: Darren Baker, 15; Newscom: Joe Russo/
imageSPACE/Sipa USA, 17; Shutterstock: Aleshyn_
Andrei, 7, Armin Staudt, 23, BAKOUNINE, bottom 31,
Brainsil, 38, CREATISTA, 33, Daniel M Ernst, 37, Darren
Baker, 45, Dragon Images, 27, Everett Collection, bottom
41, Fabio Diena, 29, Ivan Svyatkovsky, Cover, 1, Lopolo,
18, michaeljung, 21, Monkey Business Images, 5, 24,
28, top 31, top 41, 43, Prostock-studio, 35, Rawpixel.
com, 3, 6, 14, 19, solominviktor, 13, UfaBizPhoto, 16,
wavebreakmedia, 9, Who is Danny, 11, zieusin, 42

Printed and bound in the United States of America.
PA49

TABLE OF CONTENTS

Chapter 1

The Hot Seat 4

Chapter 2

Worrying and What to Do About It 8

Chapter 3

Perfectly Imperfect You. 12

Chapter 4

Navigating Daily Life 20

Chapter 5

Getting Involved: A Beginner's Guide. 26

Chapter 6

Let Your Voice Shine 36

Ask for Help 46

Read More. 47

Internet Sites. 47

Index 48

CHAPTER 1

>>>>>>>>>

THE
HOT SEAT

It's the first day of school. Everyone must tell the class a few things they did over the summer. One by one, each student says something. The other students watch and listen. It seems pretty simple, but as it gets closer to your turn, you start feeling hot and a little nauseous. Just the thought of speaking in front of the whole class makes you sick. Does this sound like you?

Many people feel this way when they have to speak in front of others. Speaking up in front of just a few people can be hard for some. If you're shy or introverted, talking to others or public speaking can be a nerve-racking experience. It can be difficult to get over your fears, but it's not impossible. So how do you overcome this fear? You just need to find some tools you can use that fit your way of communicating.

WHY ARE YOU QUIET?

Different people are quiet for different reasons. Psychologists have three basic reasons that people might be quiet:

- ☐ You might be shy. This means you might be uncomfortable around new people or people in general. You may also be afraid of people judging you when you talk.

- ☐ If you have extreme fear of social situations, you may have social anxiety. People with social anxiety might even avoid social situations altogether.

- ☐ If you're introverted, being around people for too long can drain you and make you tired. You'll likely be quieter around others while you feel this way. Then you might need time alone to recharge.

Your quietness can come from one or more of these reasons. Try not to worry too much about what makes you quiet. Just know that whatever the reason, it is possible to find your voice and speak up when you need to and want to. Many people have at least some fear of and anxiety about speaking up. It's normal, and it's OK. Learning more about these fears and anxieties is the first step in finding your voice.

CHAPTER 2
WORRYING
AND WHAT TO DO
ABOUT IT

>>>>>>>>

Worry is similar to anxiety. To worry means you feel concern about something. Everybody worries about friends, school, and other parts of life. Worrying from time to time is normal and healthy. It can be good in small doses and at the right times. If you have an upcoming test, worrying about it can help motivate you to study.

Some people feel worry and anxiety in their body, through their heartbeat, breath, a fluttery feeling in the stomach, and more. That anxiety grows and grows. It becomes constant and it leads to problems. How do you know if those problems have taken over? Ask yourself a few questions:

☐ Is being on time your constant fear, even though you're always early?

☐ Do you stay up at night thinking about whether or not you'll do well on a test at school the next day, even when you always ace your tests?

☐ Does finding friends at lunchtime always worry you, even though it usually works out fine?

☐ Do you keep thinking about little mistakes you may have made in the past? Do you have a hard time getting your mind off those mistakes?

If you feel like your anxiety is impacting your everyday life, consider talking to a trusted adult. An adult can help you figure out if you need professional help. He or she can direct you to the right place to get it. You can also contact one of the help lines listed on page 46.

ANXIETY TRIGGERS AND HOW TO DEAL WITH THEM

Does the thought of getting called on in class scare you? Or maybe parties are your trigger? Whatever makes you feel most anxious is your anxiety trigger. Do you know what your triggers are? Knowing them is the first step in dealing with your anxiety.

For some people, certain social situations cause a lot of anxiety and worry. You might feel tense and find it difficult to talk in these situations. It can get worse in a new school when you need to meet new people. Figuring out what situations trigger your anxiety can help you better deal with them.

Keep a journal to help you figure out what is causing your worry and anxiety. Write down these experiences each day. Where were you? How did you feel? How long did those feelings last? After a few weeks, you may begin to notice a pattern. Certain events or situations will make you feel worse. Being mindful of them will help you recognize your anxiety as it happens. Instead of getting caught up in your anxiety, you can take steps right away to minimize those feelings.

Try some things to keep yourself calm:

☐ Take care of your body. Eat healthy foods and get plenty of sleep. Get moving too. Exercise not only helps your body, but it also helps your mind. A healthy, rested body will help your mind feel at ease.

☐ Tell someone how you're feeling. Find a friend or a relative you trust. Talk about your anxiety and worries with that person. Saying it out loud may make your anxiety seem less scary. It will relieve some pressure you feel too.

☐ Focus on your breathing. Breathe deeply and slowly, in and out. Breathe in through your nose and out through your mouth. Think about each breath. You will soon feel your body and mind slowing down too.

>>>>>> What's a Panic Attack?

You're facing the class, about to read your report. Suddenly your heart starts pounding really hard. Sweat rolls down your forehead. Then it feels really hard to breathe. Are you having a heart attack? Probably not. Most likely what you're feeling is a panic attack. Your physical symptoms are the result of extreme anxiety. It's scary having a panic attack, especially the first time. But many people have them. They usually peak 10 minutes after you start feeling them. Then they start to go away. If you know you are having a panic attack, remind yourself that it will pass. Breathe through it and accept it. This will help your panic attack stop faster than if you try to fight it. If you think you've had a panic attack, you should also tell a trusted adult.

CHAPTER 3
PERFECTLY
IMPERFECT YOU

>>>>>>>>>>>

"I'm so weird."

"Why did I say that?"

"I look so bad."

Do these negative thoughts or ones like them ever creep into your mind? If they keep repeating, you'll start to believe them. These negative thoughts are part of feeling insecure about yourself. If you feel insecure, you lack confidence in yourself. You think you're not good enough, not smart enough, not enough in different ways. This can stop you from being yourself. It can also be one reason you speak up less around others.

Feeling insecure is something everyone deals with. But the thing is, nobody's perfect. When you're focused on your insecurities, it can be easy to forget the good things about yourself. Don't let yourself focus on all the negative. You are in control of your thoughts. You have the power to break the habit of negative thoughts, and there are a lot of ways to do so.

FROM THE NEGATIVE TO THE POSITIVE

Make a list of positive things about yourself. Do you have mad math skills? Are you great at crafts? Do you excel at soccer or another sport? Add to your list as you think of these things. You can look at it later when you're having negative thoughts about yourself.

When negative thoughts start taking over, notice them. You can stop them right then. Think of something positive from your list you know you can do. If you start repeating the positives over and over, you will begin to believe them. They will crowd out the negative thoughts. Soon you'll be able to break the pattern of negative self-talk.

Sometimes your insecurities get bigger around certain people or in certain situations. Do you know someone who often makes negative comments about how you look? Do the comments cause you to feel badly just being around that person? Maybe that person is part of the popular group, so you stick around just to feel popular too. Usually people who are negative to others are deeply insecure. They try to make themselves feel better by putting you down. That's not a healthy friendship. You need to take care of yourself and pay attention to how you feel. Try to surround yourself with people who make you feel good. They'll remind you of what's good in yourself.

LIFE TIP

Write some of the positive things about yourself on sticky notes or note cards. Tape them up around your bedroom or other places you might see them. Seeing them frequently will help you believe them and remember them when you're feeling negative about yourself.

DEALING WITH PERFECTIONISM

Another thing that may be holding your voice back is perfectionism. You should always try to be the best that you can be. But for some people, that means trying to be perfect—all the time. Some people never want to make mistakes and always want to say the right things. There's just one problem with this, though. Perfection does not exist. Trying to be perfect all the time may prevent you from doing a lot of things. If you are worried about always saying the perfect thing, perfectionism may stop you from talking to others.

Perfectionism may work for you sometimes, but we all make mistakes. If you hold yourself to such high standards, you can feel like a failure if you make just one mistake. There are some things you can do to deal with perfectionism when talking with others. Try playing the "what if" game. Ask yourself *"What if no one likes my idea?"* Then answer it, *"They'll probably just want to hear more ideas."* The "what if" game forces you to think of the worst thing that could happen, and it's probably not so bad. It can help you trust yourself to say what you want to say, without worrying as much about the results. Over time you'll worry less about saying the perfect thing. You'll start saying what you mean and feel more confident when you speak.

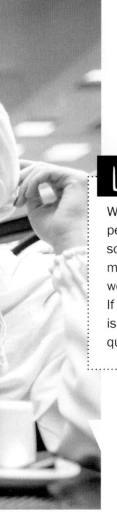

LIFE TIP

Watch how other people react when someone makes a mistake. They probably won't even notice. If they do, the mistake is usually forgotten quickly.

>>> Misty Copeland

When Misty Copeland started dancing at age 13, there were very few African American ballerinas. She had no idea that one day she would become the first African American principal dancer with the American Ballet Theatre (ABT). After joining the ABT, her body developed. She was curvy. She no longer had the "perfect" ballerina body. Copeland felt the need to be perfect. She became quieter and more nervous at the ABT. But her friends outside of ballet didn't have such strict rules about how their bodies should look. Being around these positive people helped Copeland let go of the perfectionism that was holding her back. She began dancing more confidently. She rose up in the company to the principal position.

MAKING MISTAKES

Another way to break the pattern of perfectionism is to allow yourself to make mistakes. You can do this by trying something new. Is there a craft you've been meaning to try? Or maybe you've been thinking about trying out for the track team.

You will likely make mistakes when you are doing something for the very first time. But instead of seeing those mistakes as failures, flip your perspective. A mistake is an opportunity to learn. It teaches you what doesn't work. The next time you try, you'll know what to avoid and probably do a better job.

This applies to conversations too. Observe what works and what doesn't when you talk with others. Make a mental note. Don't feel badly about yourself. Just use what worked in your next conversation.

Allowing yourself to make mistakes can be scary. Ease into it. Know that changing your perspective is a long-term process. Over time and with regular work, you'll see that mistakes are just part of the process of trying. As you try talking with others more, your confidence will grow and you'll feel better about yourself.

CHAPTER 4

NAVIGATING DAILY LIFE

>>>>>>>>>>

Even if you're quiet, you still need to get out into the world. Everyone needs to communicate with others. But the world can be a busy, noisy, in-your-face kind of place. Lots of stimulating things happen all around you. Whether it's at school, the store, or a party, that stimulation can get overwhelming for anyone.

Some people are very sensitive to the world's stimulation. That stimulation ranges from background noises to the number of people around. Science shows that the nervous systems of some people react more than others. Some people need less time in stimulating environments because they absorb more from their surroundings. That means that too much time in overstimulating environments can be overwhelming.

Everyone reacts to overstimulation in different ways. Some people might just shut down. They may stop talking altogether, feel anxious, and want to leave right away. Learn to recognize when you are overstimulated. Keep track of these instances in a journal. Write down details of the situation and how you felt. Knowing what triggers your overstimulation will help you better prepare and deal with it in the future.

QUIET TIME

One way to prepare for overstimulation is to calm your mind before it even happens. After school and on the weekends, make sure you get in some quiet time. How do you do that? Try reading for a half hour in your room. Close the curtains, shut the door, and make it nice and quiet. If you share your room, find a quiet space in your house or yard. Keep the stimulation low. You'll feel some of the day's stress melt away.

Being in nature can also help keep you calm and more focused. Go outside and focus on the trees and plants. Watch the insects scurry on the ground or buzz from plant to plant. Listen to the wind blowing through the leaves or the birds singing. Go for a bike ride with a friend.

Meditation is another way to calm your mind. When you meditate, you sit still, close your eyes, and focus your mind. You think about taking each breath, in and out. That's all you think about. Instead of letting your mind move from thought to thought, focus on what's happening right then. This gives your brain a break.

SCHOOL–DAY BREAKS

School can be especially draining for some people. It's hectic moving from class to class in packed hallways. Everyone's talking, and it can be super noisy. It can be intimidating and overwhelming navigating through each school day. How do you not only get through the day, but also thrive and enjoy it?

If possible, find some quiet spots in your school where you can rest from the commotion of public areas. If you have a break during the day, go sit in the library and read.

But you can't spend all day in those quiet spots. In class, you need to participate and be heard. Speaking up in class might be hard for you, but you can try some things to make it easier. If you know what the class is going to talk about that day, make notes of things you'd like to say. If you go blank when it's your turn to speak, glance at your notes. They will remind you of what you want to say. Sitting in the front row can help. That way when you speak, you won't see everyone looking at you.

While you're speaking, remember to think positively. If you mess up or get a question wrong, that's OK. Most people will forget by the end of class.

LIFE TIP

Make some small speaking goals to start. Maybe you can ask one question in class. Then gradually work your way up to bigger goals.

CHAPTER 5
GETTING INVOLVED: A BEGINNER'S GUIDE

>>>>>>>>

Even if you do like alone time, everyone needs some social time too. There isn't one correct way to be social. You don't need a million friends, and you don't need to be in crowds to be part of the fun.

It's easiest to start with making just one friend. Having one-on-one conversations is the first step to finding your voice. But if you have a hard time speaking to others, how do you make a friend? It's not easy for everyone. Start with small goals. Say hello to someone new each day. Give someone a compliment. See if you have something in common with that person.

Then try talking about those common interests. Asking questions is a great way to get a conversation going. Be a good listener. Follow up with more questions. Over time, the conversation will get a little easier as you get to know each other better. If you really like each other, that person may become a good friend. It takes time and regular work to make and keep friends. But a real friend is worth so much.

GROUPS, CLUBS, AND CLASSES

One way to find people with common interests is by getting involved with groups, clubs, or classes. You just need to find the ones that are right for you. Finding the right kind of group or club is key to being more confident in social situations. You'll meet new people and expand your social circle. You'll be trying something new too. This helps you get out of your social comfort zone.

So how do you find the right groups or classes? Really think about what you love to do. Brainstorm a list and write down everything that comes to mind. Do you love robots, cooking, or reading? Whatever it is that you like, there's bound to be a club, class, or a group that focuses on what you love. If you join one, you'll find other people who love what you do. Having a common interest makes chatting with others easier. You already know something that they love, and that makes for a great conversation starter. If there isn't something you can join, try starting your own club.

>>>> Beyoncé

You've heard her songs and have probably seen videos of her strong stage performances. Beyoncé is one of the most famous singers and songwriters in the world. Her onstage persona is bold and fearless. But offstage, Beyoncé is quiet and shy. Yet this superstar has found that performing helps her become more self-confident and shine. In an interview she said, "I always try to be myself. Ever since I was an introverted kid, I'd get on stage and be able to break out of my shell."

HANDLING LARGE GROUPS

You may be great at socializing one-on-one. It's a quieter way of being social. You can focus on one person and talk about topics in-depth. And you might have a good friend who you always like to hang out with. But larger groups might be harder for you to handle. There are many people to focus on and the conversation tends to be more small talk than deep conversations. But being in larger groups can be fun. So how can you find ways to socialize in large groups while still being yourself and feeling comfortable?

One way is to bring your comfort zone with you! If you have a good friend, partner up with that person when you're in a larger group. You'll have someone there you feel comfortable with. It may help you feel more at ease with the other people you meet.

Large groups can be loud and overwhelming. It might be better for you to ease into the crowd. Start at the edges of the group, talking to a few people. Then slowly make your way into the thick of it. You'll ease into the group and the stimulation that comes with it.

LIFE TIP

When you're around crowds, try taking little breaks when you can. Go to the bathroom. Find a hallway away from the crowd. Rest your mind for a minute and then head back to the crowd when you're ready.

>>>>> Emma Watson

Emma Watson is famous actor. She identifies as an introvert. She never liked going to parties and thought something was wrong with herself. But she eventually came to accept her quietness as a strength, not a weakness. She says, "The truth is that I'm genuinely a shy, socially awkward, introverted person. At a big party, I'm like Bambi in the headlights. It's too much stimulation for me, which is why I end up going to the bathroom! I need time outs!"

YOUR EXIT PLAN

You're out and about and testing your party socializing skills. You're having fun and meeting new people, and even getting in some quality small talk. Then suddenly you've had enough. You just need to be alone. You can't think of one more thing to say and even smiling politely is hard. You don't want to be rude, but you feel like you need to leave—like *now*. What do you do?

Pay attention to that feeling. It's there for a reason. Your mind is telling you something important. Ignoring it won't do you any good. If you force yourself to stay, you may not be your best self. You may appear moody, mad, or tired, even when that's not how you feel at all. It's just your energy is low and you need some quiet time to get it back up.

Once you recognize that you need to leave, get moving on your exit plan. Politely explain to others that you need to leave. You can say, "I'm feeling tired. I think I'm going to leave." If you're at a party, thank your host. Then just leave and don't feel badly about it.

LIFE TIP

If you're worried you may want to leave a social event early, plan ahead. You can set a time to have a parent pick you up before you even get there.

>>>> Quiz: What Would You Do?

How would you handle leaving each situation in this quiz? Test yourself and see
what may be seen as polite or impolite ways to leave.

1. You're at your friend's birthday party. You've had food, cake, and lots of laughs,
but now you want to go. But nobody else has left. You:
   a) Slip out the back door when no one is looking.
   b) Tell the host that you had so much fun, but you need to leave.

2. You're at a concert with a friend and it's not over yet. But the crowd is too much
and you feel overwhelmed. Your friend wants to stay. You:
   a) Tell your friend she has to leave right then or you'll be mad.
   b) Suggest standing at the edge of the crowd where there are fewer people until
      the concert is over.

3. There's a big festival where you've met up with a bunch of people. After an hour,
you need to get out of there. You don't want any pressure to stay, so you:
   a) Make up a big excuse about having a sudden stomachache.
   b) Just tell one person in the group that you're going home and quietly leave.

If you answered mostly A's, you might risk upsetting people when you leave when you leave.
Making threats or lying about how you feel are not good ways to get out of being social. If you
answered mostly B's, think about more considerate ways to leave.

CONNECTING WITH CREATIVITY

Is it possible to get out and be involved without chatting for hours? Yes! Everyone is creative in one way or another. You might like painting, cooking, or building toy trains. Paint a picture that means something to you. Write a story about an important moment in your life. Make some music filled with feeling. Or find some other form of creativity that fits you. Maybe it's photography, poetry, pottery, baking, woodworking, or something else. There are tons of ways to be creative.

Once you feel good about what you're making, you can share your passion with others. See if there is a community group you can join with similar artists. Submit your artwork to public art shows. Ask an art teacher at school about any public displays. Have an adult help you make an online portfolio of your art to share with others. An adult can also help you use social media to promote your art and connect with other artists. If you're a writer, ask an adult to help you publish your stories with magazines or websites. Soon you may develop a community of fans and friends.

CHAPTER 6

LET YOUR VOICE SHINE

>>>>>>>>

As a quiet person, you probably aren't the loudest one in the room. You may not state your thoughts and feelings as much as other people do. That's OK, but sometimes you need to use your voice when it is important. When you clearly state your needs, feelings, and opinions, you are being assertive. It's not always easy to do this.

As a quiet person, maybe you've been too passive. Passive people do not state their opinions. They might speak quietly and not look at other people when they talk.

On the other hand, aggressive people might state their opinions. However, they might interrupt and talk over people, speak really loudly, and glare at you while saying what they think. Passive-aggressive people are harder to spot. They won't tell you exactly what they think. Instead, they'll try to hurt you in ways that are hard to recognize. They might stop saying hello to you or give you a compliment that's really an insult in disguise.

It's healthy to voice your opinions in an assertive way. You'll let others know how you feel without being mean about it. You'll feel better for letting those feelings out and other people will know how you'd like to be treated.

So how do you know when to be assertive and when to let things slide? If something makes you feel uncomfortable or unsure, you should speak up. What if someone at school wants you to write on the bathroom wall with her? You want to stay friends with her, but you know vandalizing the bathroom is wrong. You can say, "I don't want to get in trouble." Or even, "I really need to get started on my homework." What if someone tries to bully you on the bus? He always calls you a name. It's mean and makes you feel badly. You could try ignoring him. That might make him stop. Or you could confront him and tell him to stop. Try not to let his words bother you, though. If he won't leave you alone, report him to the school.

When you are assertive, you clearly let others know your thoughts. If they get mad at you, that's OK. Never let someone make you go against your morals or feel badly. Being assertive sets up your boundaries. These are your limits. They protect you from doing things you don't want to do. Good friends will respect your boundaries. They won't try to make you cross them.

LIFE TIP

Learning to be assertive takes some time. Try practicing saying some assertive things in front of a mirror.

BECOMING A QUIET LEADER

Being assertive helps you overcome challenges when dealing with one person. But it can also help you become better at dealing with groups of people. This can set you up for being a great leader. As a quiet person, you may not think that leading others comes naturally to you. It might sound a bit scary, but that's a challenge you can overcome. While you may lead differently than an extroverted person, you should know that quiet people have great leadership skills too.

A good leader doesn't overpower the other people in a group. A good leader listens to others. And many quiet people are excellent listeners. Listening to others and encouraging people to voice their thoughts lets them know that you respect their opinions. It shows you think they have something valuable to add to the group. If people know you respect them, they will respect you more as a leader too.

Quiet leaders often focus well and stay dedicated to their work. They lead by example, which inspires others to work in the same way.

>>>>> Barack Obama

As U.S. president, some people saw Barack Obama as a quiet leader. Many people believe he is an introvert. He often preferred time alone to work and think. Yet he used his voice to become a powerful leader. He believes a person's voice has power. He said during a speech, "One voice can change a room, and if one voice can change a room, then it can change a city, and if it can change a city, it can change a state, and if it changes a state, it can change a nation, and if it can change a nation, it can change the world. Your voice can change the world."

FACING THE CROWD

Even as a quiet leader, you may still feel nervous stepping into the spotlight and speaking publicly. Most people are nervous getting in front of others. With all eyes on you, it's hard to know where to look. And it's not easy speaking to others without getting a response. You might think: *Am I making sense? Do they understand me?* But being a little nervous is good. It means that you really care about being a good speaker and getting your message across. You may not be brilliant at it the first time you try, but it will likely be much easier to try the second, third, and fourth time. With practice you will improve.

Some things will help you feel more at ease once you're facing a crowd. First, be prepared. Know your topic inside and out and bring notes with you that you can look at when needed. You can also practice what you want to say in front of a mirror or other people you know well. Ask for advice on what needs to improve and what sounded great. Then change what you think needs to be changed and highlight the good things. When you are in front of the crowd, remember to smile. It will help you feel more relaxed and confident.

LIFE TIP

If possible, visit the room where you will be speaking beforehand. Being familiar with the space will help you feel more comfortable.

QUIET CONFIDENCE

Becoming more comfortable with yourself and more confident takes time. Be patient with yourself. As you make mistakes, remember that the important thing is to learn from them. Don't give up. It's all an important part of finding your voice. And once you've found your voice, you'll be able to share all the wonderful things about yourself.

Set some socializing goals and get started on accomplishing them. You'll gain confidence as you try new ways to connect with other people, and you'll realize what quiet strengths you possess.

Quiet or not, everyone has something important to say. Your thoughts, opinions, and ideas are valuable and should be heard. Remember that you have much to offer the world, and you can find ways to do it that fit your style. Just stay true to who you are, and speak up in your own way. Let your unique voice be heard!

ASK FOR HELP

If you believe you're suffering from anxiety, depression, or another mental health issue or are the victim of bullying, ask for help. Reach out to a teacher, school counselor, parent, or another trusted adult. Doctors, psychologists, and social workers are available to get you the help you need. You can also reach out to one of these organizations below.

National Safe Place
provides immediate help and safety to any youth in crisis
https://www.nationalsafeplace.org/
Text SAFE and your current location to 4HELP (44357) for immediate help.

National Suicide Prevention
national network of local crisis centers that provide free and confidential
    support
https://suicidepreventionlifeline.org/
800-273-8255

Stomp Out Bullying!
national nonprofit dedicated to preventing bullying, cyberbullying, and other
    digital abuse
http://stompoutbullying.org/

Teen Line
teen-to-teen hotline for when you just need someone to talk to
https://teenlineonline.org/
310-855-4673
Text TEEN to 839863.

Trevor Project
leading national organization providing crisis intervention and suicide prevention
    services to LGBTQ youth
https://www.thetrevorproject.org
866-488-7386
Text START to 678678.

READ MORE

Cain, Susan. *Quiet Power: The Secret Strengths of Introverts*. New York: Dial Books for Young Readers, 2016.

Roberts, Emily. *Express Yourself: A Teen Girl's Guide to Speaking Up and Being Who You Are*. Oakland, Calif.: Instant Help Books, an imprint of New Harbinger Publications, 2015.

Sack, Rebekah. *The Young Adult's Guide to Saying No: The Complete Guide to Building Confidence and Finding Your Assertive Voice*. Ocala, Fl.: Atlantic Publishing Group, 2016.

INTERNET SITES

Use FactHound to find Internet sites related to this book.

Visit *www.facthound.com*

Just type in 9780756560218 and go.

 Check out projects, games and lots more at **www.capstonekids.com**

INDEX

anxiety, 7, 8, 9, 10, 20

being assertive, 36, 39, 40
Beyoncé, 29
breathing, 8, 10, 11, 22

class participation, 25
communication, 20
confidence, 12, 16, 17, 19, 28, 29, 44
conversation, 29
conversations, 18, 26, 30
Copeland, Misty, 17
creativity, 34

exercise, 10
exit plans, 32

fear, 4, 6, 7, 10
friendships, 15

goals, 25, 26, 44

healthy eating, 10

insecurities, 12, 15
introversion, 4, 6, 29, 31, 41

journaling, 10, 20

leadership, 40, 41, 42

making friends, 26
meditation, 22

nausea, 4
negative thoughts, 12, 14, 15
nervous system, the, 20

Obama, Barack, 41
opinions, 36, 44

panic attacks, 11
perfectionism, 16, 17, 18
public speaking, 4, 42

quiet time, 22, 24, 32

shyness, 4, 6, 31
sleep, 10
social anxiety, 6
socializing in groups, 30, 32
socializing one-on-one, 30
stimulation, 20, 22
stress, 22
sweat, 11

trying new things, 18, 28-29

Watson, Emma, 31
worry, 8, 10, 16